Mind Your PETS

An Effective Guide to Build Mannerisms in Children

Deepshree Jhingran Sharma

Made with ❤ on the Notion Press Platform

www.notionpress.com

This book is dedicated to my father

Lt. Shri Anand Jhingran

11th Dec 1936 -22nd August 2019

Who has been a real inspiration behind this book.

A reserved soul because he always believed...

Action speaks Louder than words, a strict disciplinarian and proved it too.

Contents

Foreword

This piece of work is solely an individual effort. This is the crux of my experience over the years in teaching and training kids of all age groups.

In my entire teaching, training, and counseling career, I have witnessed that the world is getting busy, and I find children do not have access to their parent's company as and when required.

There is a constant tussle between the children and parents to develop good relationships.

Parents expect their children to be well-behaved at home, school, with peers, friends, teachers and other family members but fail to provide quality and sufficient time to incorporate the same into them.

I am hopeful, that this work will undoubtedly impact readers' minds and they will nurture their children to make the world a better place and they will surely start understanding their child in a new way.

Date 14th, November '23

Preface

The idea of this book struck with the changing trends of the society.

Indian culture and traditions flourished in a close-knit society where joint family was the foundation of all values and good manners. The children learned it all with each other, cousins were their best friends, and above all the grandparent's bedtime stories filled up the gaps.

Advancement modernization and urbanization reduced the joint families to unitary families, gadgets replaced friends and cousins. To meet both ends, parents started working leaving the children at the mercy of caretakers and gadgets.

The value of education became materialistic. The children became demanding to such an extent that the parents feared if they did not fulfill the demands of their children they may take drastic steps, like leaving the home or harming one's own life.

PREFACE

Children today are loud-mouthed, and do not realize the difference between the young and old. Seldomly do they understand when to speak, how to speak, and what tone to use.

My day-to-day experience in coming across such incidents inspired me to pen it down all.

Train them young. The future depends on how we prepare ourselves today, with this aim in mind this book was conceived.

Deepshree Jhingran Sharma

22nd August 2023

Acknowledgments

My sincere thanks goes to all my teaching and training sessions over the years who have been a real source of inspiration behind this book.

To all my students who have suffered the lacune due to an inappropriate nurturing of their childhood.

To both my sons Sankalp and Sanskar who have been constant specimens for all the tricks I tried over them to get the desired behavioural changes in them.

To my husband Dinesh Chand Sharma for not believing on my experiments and who always challanged by putting forward his logical and analytical arguments to discipline the children.

To my mother Mrs Lakshmi Jhingran, who instilled the good values to be worldly wise and religion to understand the difference between the right and the wrong.

I am no psychologist, just a mother striving for well-behaved, disciplined, and humble human beings. I feel responsible to fulfill my duty in upbringing the children in the right way who later in life can be an asset to both family and the society.

This book is therefore just a small step to help other mothers with the same aim and desire.

I would also like to extend my gratitude to all my readers for accepting the same and be benefitted by it.

Chapter: 1

Manners Maketh a Man

"A parent can give a child no greater gift than good manners."

–Hakim

In the present day, there are many parameters for determining success. Apart from good education, appropriate skills, a pleasing personality, and excellent communication skill, many individuals happen to fail in accruing the desired results. The tone of your conversation matters.

Manners are social lubrication, which, without a doubt are exhibited in your behavior.

The one major distinct quality between successful and unsuccessful people is that most successful people are grateful for everything they have in life, whereas unsuccessful people are never grateful for anything.

We often fail to express gratitude. Parents bring us into this world, all the time we have parents in our homes we take them for granted and don't value them. We fail to take care of them. Alas, when they leave us and are far away, we recollect their love and care for us and then cry for them if only we had valued and taken care of them when they were alive, they would have been with us even longer.

Similarly, we often forget the fourth parameter to success: the use of four known Golden Words Please, Excuse me, Thank you, and Sorry (PETS).

Good manners can be determined by how often you use these four words. Everyone likes children who practice good manners in their day-to-day life. The strong scaffolds for the building blocks of proper etiquette and good manners lie within the magic words "please", "excuse me", "thank you", and "I'm sorry". These are the powerful words and phrases that should be taught to children from an early age.

The right to Speech is our Fundamental Right, does not mean that we misuse it. As our elders in the olden time said first think (socho), then weigh (tolo), and then speak (bolo).

The advent of mobile phones and their marketing strategies (unlimited talk time) and punch lines (walk while you talk and talk while you walk endlessly) has reversed the order. Now the people first speak (bolo), and then they weigh (tolo) and realize that the blunder has been committed, and by the time they think (socho) the harm is already done.

Chapter 2:

Use: Please to show Respect

"How you make others feel about themselves says a lot about you."

Anonamous

Yet another day, Gilbert returned from school with a big face and threw his bag to one side, and flung his shoes to the other.

Mom noticed this strange behavior but remained quiet, and handed a glass of cold water to him. She quietly picked up the scattered things and placed them in their respective places, left the room closing the door noiselessly.

Later in the evening Mom brought a glass of milk with his favorite cookies and sat down beside him on the sofa.

Gilbert sipped his milk half-heartedly. Mom placed her hand over his shoulder affectionately and asked what was the matter.

Gilbert lazily slipped into Mom's lap and said he had a bad day at school. He further said that he was offended as the teacher scolded him before the entire class because he asked her to correct his unchecked notebook. Mom was perplexed and asked him to narrate what exactly happened.

Gilbert gathered courage and said that he was late in submitting his homework notebook last week and today he said to his teacher that "Ma'am you did not check my notebook." Instantly ma'am got angry and gave me a stern look. I failed to understand why she behaved so.

Mom thought for a while and said that both the sentence formation and your tone of speaking were inappropriate.

This perplexed little Gilbert further.

She explained the statement "Ma'am you did not check my notebook.", was a rude statement and did not reflect request rather it had an accusation.

Why would a teacher not check your notebook, she does not have any personal grudge against you, and you are a well-behaved child?

Mom asked her son to rethink and asked him to recall why his notebook remained unchecked and the teacher got annoyed.

Gilbert thought for a while and feeling sorry he confessed to Mom that day of all the other students submitted their notebooks he had forgotten to take his notebook and therefore he missed the submissions.

There you are so it was your mistake of not submitting your work on time.

"What should I do now, asked Gilbert?"

Mom suggested just reframe your statement, and be apologetic in your attitude and requesting in your tone.

The next day, Gilbert gathered all his courage and approached his teacher, and said:

"Ma'am I am sorry, “I forgot the date of submission as a result my notebook remained unchecked, will you please correct my notebook I assure you this shall not be repeated in the future."

Gilbert was astonished to see the teacher's reaction she not only accepted his notebook but also patted his head affectionately and said better be careful next time.

Now let's analyze the two statements – the first one was short and direct but it was a complaint and sounded rude. While the second statement was apologetic, precisely stated the reason, and expressed regret for committing a mistake, there was a polite request to do the needful and an assurance of not repeating the same. Adding the two words "Sorry" and "Please" created the magic.

These kinds of incidences are being repeated around us everywhere and within all relations. Today we talk too much but forget where and to whom are we speaking. To be short and quick we land up to be rude and blunt, using a wrong tone.

The word please in the English language was borrowed from the French language 'plaisir' way back in the 14th century, the verb means "to be able to agree to someone" or to "satisfy someone delightfully." "Please: shows respect and enables one person's worth as a human being.

We were graded for Good manners and right conduct by teachers in the school in our childhood.

'Please' when used either at the beginning, in the middle, or at the end of a sentence, can create magic as in the case of Gilbert because it can change the tone of your conversation and turn an order into a request.

The following personality traits are exhibited if you use Please in your conversation:

A respectful request is put forward before another individual and it enables the person whether he wants to respond to your request or not.

This also ensures that you do not consider yourself superior to the other person, rather you make him feel comfortable.

Eventually, your request will be granted.

Chapter 3:

Use: Excuse Me for Self-Respect

"The art of dealing with children might be defined as knowing what not to say."

A.S Neil

Gilbert was an innocent introvert child and found it very difficult to initiate a conversation leave aside with strangers but even with his friends. At times even if he meekly tried to get into a conversation he was very easily and conveniently dominated by the others and then failed to resume.

On the PTM day, Gilbert's teacher discussed his introvert nature with his mother. She said that he fails to answer in class despite knowing the answers.

The mother was curious as Gilbert (her son) did not show any signs of excelling his performance in class.

Mother spoke to Gilbert that evening, and very innocently he said "I face three problems:

Firstly, I fail to gather the attention of others.

Secondly, I am unable to put forward my point of view before others with confidence.

Thirdly, while the others are speaking I am unable to find space for myself to intervene and become a part of the main conversation.

His mother understood the problem she introduced him to the powerful words in the English language to which 'Excuse me' topped the list.

Saying "excuse me" moves you back into social equilibrium. These two words can smooth over a mistake and gather attention from the others, it can also provide an exit, among the other tasks. It's a terrific phrase to remember when you've been surprised by a situation and are stumped on what to say.

However, understanding the use of "excuse me" can be easily learned by using it frequently.

When you use "excuse me" to get attention, the response would be "I'm sorry, yes?" When you say "excuse me" because you are in the way of someone, then the response is to move out of the way and say "I'm sorry" or "sorry".

Mother explained to Gilbert all such situations where this powerful phrase comes in handy:

When you intend to break through a conversation to ask for assistance or give instructions. e.g. "Excuse me, kind attention, please take your seats and the show is about to begin shortly.

When you want to avoid a possible misunderstanding. e.g. "Excuse me, but I misunderstood you to be someone else.

When due to an interruption, you need to get back and resume the conversation. e.g. Excuse me, "as I was saying...."

When you have missed a piece of important information or instruction and you want it to be repeated. e.g. Excuse me, "Could you please repeat the previous statement?"

When you have to exit and yet feel comfortable that you won't be leaving anyone offended. e.g. Excuse me; "May I speak to ma'am who just came into the room."

When you need to seek attention and bring an audience together. e.g. Excuse me, "we are about to begin . . . I request everyone to be seated?"

When you want to penetrate through a crowded or public place and avoid a collision, notify another that you're close and he may bump into you. e.g. Excuse me, "I'm right behind you."

Bridging situations, for instance, after a conference you are standing around a tall table with others, and the conversation has wandered far from the speaker's just-heard talk. Excuse me, I missed what was being said…

Make an interruption acceptable. During a Group Discussion when you're in the middle of a conversation, event, or at the dinner table and it's necessary to disrupt with a question or comment. The Phrase, excuse me, comes very handy Excuse me, "I'd like to make a point here."

Excuse me, but I'd like to ask . . ."

When you are dining and need to leave the table. The table is considered to be a "closed group," and when you exit, you are interrupting the occasion.

Excuse me. "You may elaborate on your reason for leaving – or not." Excuse me, "I shall be right back."

When something in a conversation or activity needs to cease.
Excuse me, "There are children in the room."

Using "Excuse Me" can be tricky, it may also express sarcasm if used without a proper tone, and it can at times be confrontational!

It can be unknowingly used when you feel defensive or surprised.

The proper and polite way to ease through the situations listed above. Learn to practice "excuse me" as the courtesy power word.

Chapter 4

Use: Thank You to show Gratitude

"As we express our gratitude, we must never forget that the highest appreciation is not to utter words, but to live by them.".

-John F Kennedy

Gilbert was astonished when his mom said thank you to the maid for putting on the fan and shutting the door after she left.

Gilbert asked his mother innocently why did you thank Shalu di, she did not bring any gift for her.

The mother understood what was wrong, she also realized her mistake. Gilbert her six-year-old son had seen and practiced speaking "Thank you only when somebody from a family or friends gave him a storybook, a chocolate or a gift on his birthday or a present on Christmas.

Never was he asked to say thank you to people who serve us in our daily life for the small little things that they do for us. For instance, picking up the newspaper from the balcony, switching on or putting off the electricity button, or for that matter even helping you arrange the scattered table.

Gilbert and many other children of his age have never been taught that Thankyou is just not spoken when someone hands you over a gift.

Thank you is one of those PETS which should be used for every little favour which is done for us by anyone around us irrespective of their age, or financial status.

Say, thank you to the maid who comes to clean your house, to your cook who feeds you delicious food every day, to your driver who opens the door of the car for you and drives you home safely, and nevertheless to your parents who have brought us in this beautiful world, to your grandparents who are the zenith of the unconditional love they bestow upon us.

Today, Gilbert understood that saying thank you is a way to express your gratitude to all those who help you lead a beautiful and comfortable life.

He promised his mom that he shall now say thank you to all those who do even the tiniest favor for him.

This myth of saying thank you for receiving a gift was broken today.

Saying "thank you" and showing appreciation acts as an effective buffer to build better relationships, according to researchers at the University of Georgia. Feelings of gratitude can also counteract the impact of conflict and negative encounters.

Thank you is the word they need to say to express gratitude towards generosity and any help they received from others unsolicited... as in the case of Gilbert whose mother practiced with all the service people around her.

What is the purpose of saying thank you to someone?

It is the simplest form of expressing gratitude.

It shows you are grateful for the favors done to you as a result of someone else's effort. It will help you to feel better and be beneficial in an unpredictable way.

People feel appreciated and loved.

Often people feel that thanking others makes them feel inferior. On the contrary, it shows a great sign of respect for another person, his time, and his presence in your life.

Saying 'thank you', people develop a feeling that they have done something to help you. This gives inner happiness to both the doer and the receiver.

Saying 'thank you' is the simplest way to say 'I appreciate you'. People also feel motivated when they are appreciated and praised. It indicates that their effort is recognized. This may even encourage them to go an extra mile. (same as in my case).

People are attracted and they are eager to help in the future willingly.

Feel good factor brings good, back to you in an unpredictable way.

Mom recalled an anecdote and narrated to Gilbert - How a thank you made her travel 34 KMs just to buy a book. Lisa made me feel important and appreciated for taking the time to visit the shop.

Days are brightened up even in the smallest way when you make someone feel important and appreciated. These two magical words "Thankyou" act as a catalyst and are more likely to pass on that feeling to others as a chain reaction. As a result, people are willing and ready to do something for you again in the future.

The attitude of gratitude is essential if you believe in the law of karma which says:

What goes around comes around.

Say Thank you to be happier and healthier

The simple act of saying 'thank you' leads you to a happier life as confirmed by studies. Express thankfulness to others, generates peace of mind and inner happiness makes others feel great, and reciprocates the same for you.

On the other hand, people who rarely say thank you to others and what they have in life are unhappy and dissatisfied.

Gratitude (Thankyou) brings abundance in life.

'Thank you', attracts people. Friends often come around when you say thank you for their presence and every little effort or when you condemn and criticize them.

Human nature is attracted to the one who spreads positive energy. Extending thanks is one such way to spread that energy, the simplest and most effective.

Above all when you take time to thank the Almighty and appreciate all the creations of God, besides the other ways of life like being kind, generous, and compassionate you attract more joy, happiness, and abundance. Being grateful for, every little thing makes you happy.

The things you are grateful for will be abundant in your life and things you are not grateful for, will get far away from your life.

Being Thankful doesn't mean that you have to say thank you every time you breathe, drink water, or time eat food. You should feel 'thankful' when you experience a 'wow' feeling, deep down from your heart.

Never underestimate the power of gratitude.

It just brings a great change to your life.

Chapter 5

Use: Sorry to Make Up for the Mistakes

"It takes a lot of courage to own up and say Sorry"

-Anonamous

Gilbert failed to understand why it was difficult for people to ask for sorry. Until one day he was taken away by a very beautiful, attractive, and expensive pen, his friend brought to school. He picked it up unnoticed and brought it home.

On reaching home he showed the same to his mother. The mother was taken aback by this deed of her son.

At first, she was furious, but keeping the tender age of her son in mind she calmed and sat beside Gilbert to make him understand that picking up other's possessions is named as stealing if done intentionally. Whereas if you had it by mistake then you should apologies and return the same.

The next day, the classmate complained to the teacher. On reaching school everyone looked at Gilbert with anxious eyes. The teacher came to the class and asked everyone to stand and own up if anyone had stolen the pen. No one including Gilbert uttered a single word. The day passed and it was time to go home when Gilbert quietly again unnoticed dropped the pen in the drawer of the teacher's table. He ran home as fast as his tiny legs could carry him.

At home, his mother asked him if he had returned the pen and said sorry to his friend.

Now Gilbert confessed to his mother that he could not gather enough courage to admit his mistake before the entire class and say sorry. He failed to understand why it was so difficult to say this tiny yet powerful word.

Mom explained to Gilbert the Importance of Saying "I'm Sorry"

An idiom 'to err is human' says it all and is universally applicable "I'm only human." It is normal for people to make mistakes. Everybody makes mistakes, no one is perfect so what you did is okay and happened by mistake. As long as you take personal responsibility for our wrongdoing.

If you say "sorry" but do not mean it or do not intend to improve your actions will cause a lack of trust to develop. When you say "I'm sorry" and admit that you did something wrong means that you have taken the first step to self-improvement.

Apologizing, is not easy for either kids or elders though it helps to repair relationships. A sincere apology helps you face people with confidence, admitting one's mistakes reveals that you're unhappy with what you did, and won't repeat the same ever. A sincere apology shows that you not only feel sorry for your actions but also want to do better. It allows the other person a chance to reprocess his feelings.

Firstly, an apology opens a dialogue between the two individuals.

Secondly, on apologizing, you acknowledge that your behaviour was unacceptable. This helps to rebuild trust and re-establish your relations with the other person.

The word 'sorry' originated from the Old English word 'sarig' which means "distressed, grieved, or full of sorrow", but, most British people use this word more casually.

Emotional Benefits of Apology: A person who has been harmed feels that he is healing emotionally when the wrongdoer acknowledges his misdeed. On receiving an apology, you no longer perceive the wrongdoer as a personal threat. Asking Sorry opens the door to forgiveness by allowing us to have empathy for the wrongdoer.

Intention and Attitude

There are two important aspects of an apology—intention, and attitude.

They are communicated non-verbally to whom you are apologizing. If you don't apologize sincerely, it is meaningless to the other person. To prove your sincerity, the desire of saying sorry must come from deep within. Never attempt an apology because someone else tells you to do it.

To ask for forgiveness, when sincere and intentional, is powerful, perhaps even life-altering, element for both the giver and the receiver.

How to prepare yourself for a Meaningful Apology?

Mom said to Gilbert if you find difficulties asking for forgiveness or saying sorry, then follow the most effective ways of the three R's: Regret, Responsibility, and Remedy.

Regret: A statement for having caused hurt or damage.

Though your intention may not have been to cause harm, you recognize that your action or inaction nevertheless did hurt a person. This regret must be communicated. Which includes an expression of empathy with an acknowledgment of the injustice you have caused to the person.

Responsibility: An acceptance of to take up the responsibility for your actions.

This means that no one else is to be blamed for the action that hurt or makes excuses for what you did. You must be clear about accepting the total responsibility of your action or inaction for an effective apology Thus, your apology needs to include a statement of responsibility.

Gilbert admitted that he had difficulty in taking responsibility for his actions.

Remedy*:* A statement of willingness to repair the situation.

You can't undo the past, however, you can repair the harm caused. Therefore, a meaningful apology needs to include a statement in which you offer restoration, or a promise to take action not to repeat similar behavior in the future.

Only when all three of these elements are present, the other person will sense that your apology is meaningful and from the core of your heart. Your effort is genuine. Don't spend all your time to figure out who is to be blamed. Lift yourself above this petty game as you have the power to rise! On the contrary, spend that time in resolving the problem. A lot will be accomplished and less time will be wasted.

The adage 'Practice makes you perfect' has to be modified to 'Perfect practice makes you perfect'. Now, each day of his life Gilbert had learned a new lesson on the basic mannerisms. He promised his mom that he would incorporate the use of PETS day in and day out.

At the same time, his mother promised him a remarkable result in his behavior and that he would be appreciated by his family, friends at home, and peers and teachers at school.

Gilbert started using these PETS everywhere he went and used please, excuse me, thank you, and sorry as and when required irrespective of the age of a person, social status, or even rich or poor.

Two months passed, and Gilbert had been not only practicing the use of PETS well but also had been using them very effectively, and it was the PTM time again.

On the PTM day, both the mother and Gilbert were ready to go. Gilbert was excited he was full of zeal, his heart happy and his face glowing. As they approached their school building and moved closer to the classroom step by step Gilbert's heart pumped leaps and bounds, because today he was not petrified of any complaints about himself or his behavior with his peers.

The teacher welcomed both the mother and the son with a very pleasant smile. Gilbert's ears anxiously waited to hear about him from the teacher's mouth. The teacher shook hands with the mother offered her to be seated and began Mrs. Smith there is a drastic change in Gilbert's behavior...

He is now a very well-behaved child. He follows basic mannerisms and has learnt to be a soft-spoken person who used an appropriate tone to speak with his elders and peers.

Mother was overwhelmed to hear these words. The teacher's words echoed into Gilbert's ears. He had learned the ways and was now a smart confident individual to be able to handle himself well before anyone.

"No one can make you feel inferior without your consent"

-Eleanor Roosevelt

www.ingramcontent.com/pod-product-compliance
Lightning Source LLC
LaVergne TN
LVHW021202160826
845679LV00024B/2216

* 9 7 9 8 8 9 1 8 6 2 8 0 7 *